FOREVER
Mark Anthony

"forever"
written by Mark Anthony.
All Rights reserved

www.markanthonypoet.com

Published by Vagabond.

No part of this publication may be copied or transmitted in any form or any fashion without written permission from the publisher.

hi@vagabond.ltd | www.vagabond.ltd

first american edition

13 12 11 10 9 8 7 6 5 4 3 2 1

for Bird

#001

What a miracle
it is
that one person
can turn
an ordinary life
into a *love* story.

– Mark Anthony

#002

I loved you
before I even knew your name;
your smile, *your voice,*
and your laughter
were already
inside my soul,
waiting
for you
to walk through
the door.

— Mark Anthony

#003

A soulmate
will never ghost you
because
they have crossed
the universe
to find you.

- Mark Anthony

#004

You're not behind.

You're not late.

You are exactly on time
for the love story
that has already
been written
just for you.

- Mark Anthony

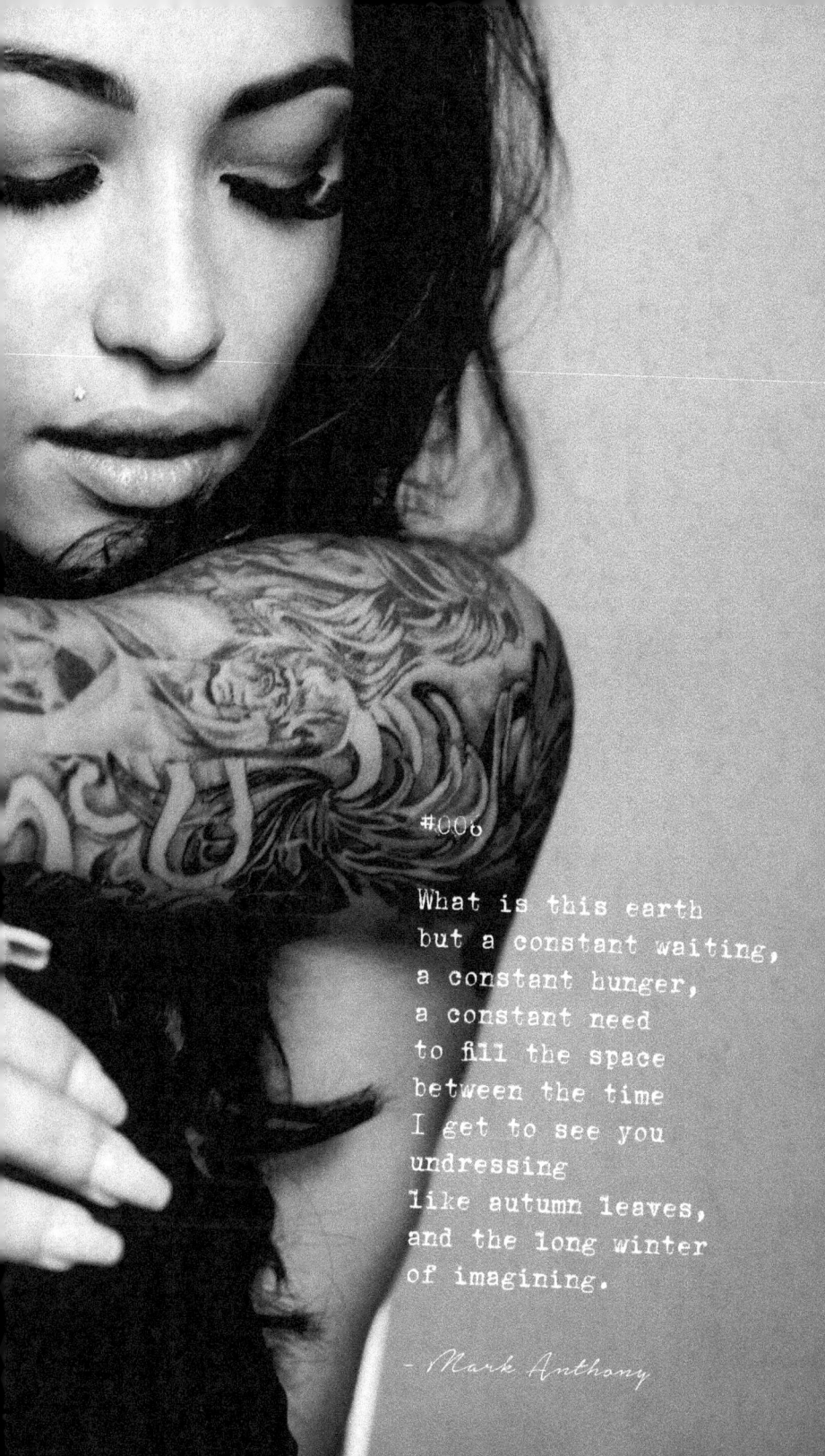

#008

Sometimes
it doesn't work out
with someone
simply because
they're a piece of shit
who deserves
a piece of shit
and you are not
a piece of shit.

- Mark Anthony

#009

Timing in love
doesn't mean
anything
if you both
don't see
just how
damn lucky
you are
to have met.

- Mark Anthony

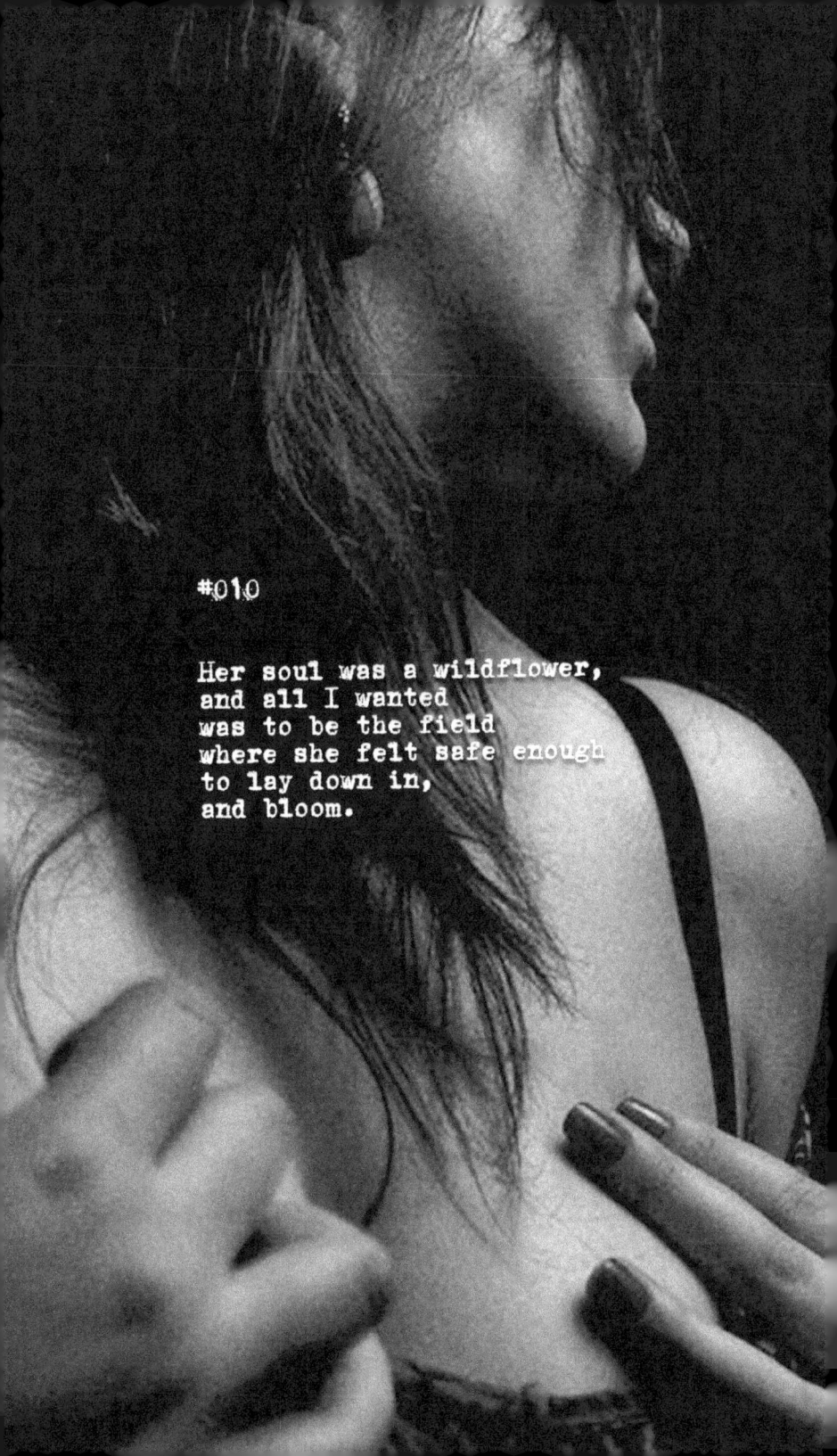

#011

There is nothing
more lonely
than being held
by somebody
who isn't really there.

- *Mark Anthony*

#012

If you tell her,
that you are
here for her,
you better mean
for all of it,
the joy, the ache,
the fire, the rain,
because real love
demands we
stay for it all,
or we will end up

with *nothing.*

- Mark Anthony

#013

One day
you'll meet somebody
who listens to you
the way the ocean
listens to the moon,
and will be forever
pulled together
by the tide.

— Mark Anthony

#014

Just in case
no one told you today,
you are worth keeping,
worth committing to,
worth making a priority,
and worth loving
the way
you deserve
to be loved.

- Mark Anthony

#015

I remember
being lonely,
and waiting for love
to walk through my door,
but by the time it did,
I had to learn
to love myself,
and appreciate
my own company.

When you
are at peace
with yourself,
when love
arrives
it will feel both
miraculous
and as normal
as ordering
a second cup of coffee
for her,
on a rainy
Tuesday morning.

- Mark Anthony

#016

No matter how beautiful
the body,
it won't last
without the beauty
of the soul.

- Mark Anthony

#017

Every "no" you've heard
was the universe protecting you
from what wasn't meant for you,
so you could be ready
for the "yes" that lasts a
lifetime.

- Mark Anthony

#018

Imagine finding great sex,
intelligent conversation,

and *laughter,*

all in the same person.

- Mark Anthony

#019

Somewhere,
someone is smiling
at the thought of you.

Even though they've never met
you,
their soul remembers
what its been missing,
and what it has been missing,
is you.

- Mark Anthony

#020

It's not too late.

You're not too broken.

Love has not forgotten your name.

Love is coming to find you.

Love is always worth the wait.

Love is always on time.

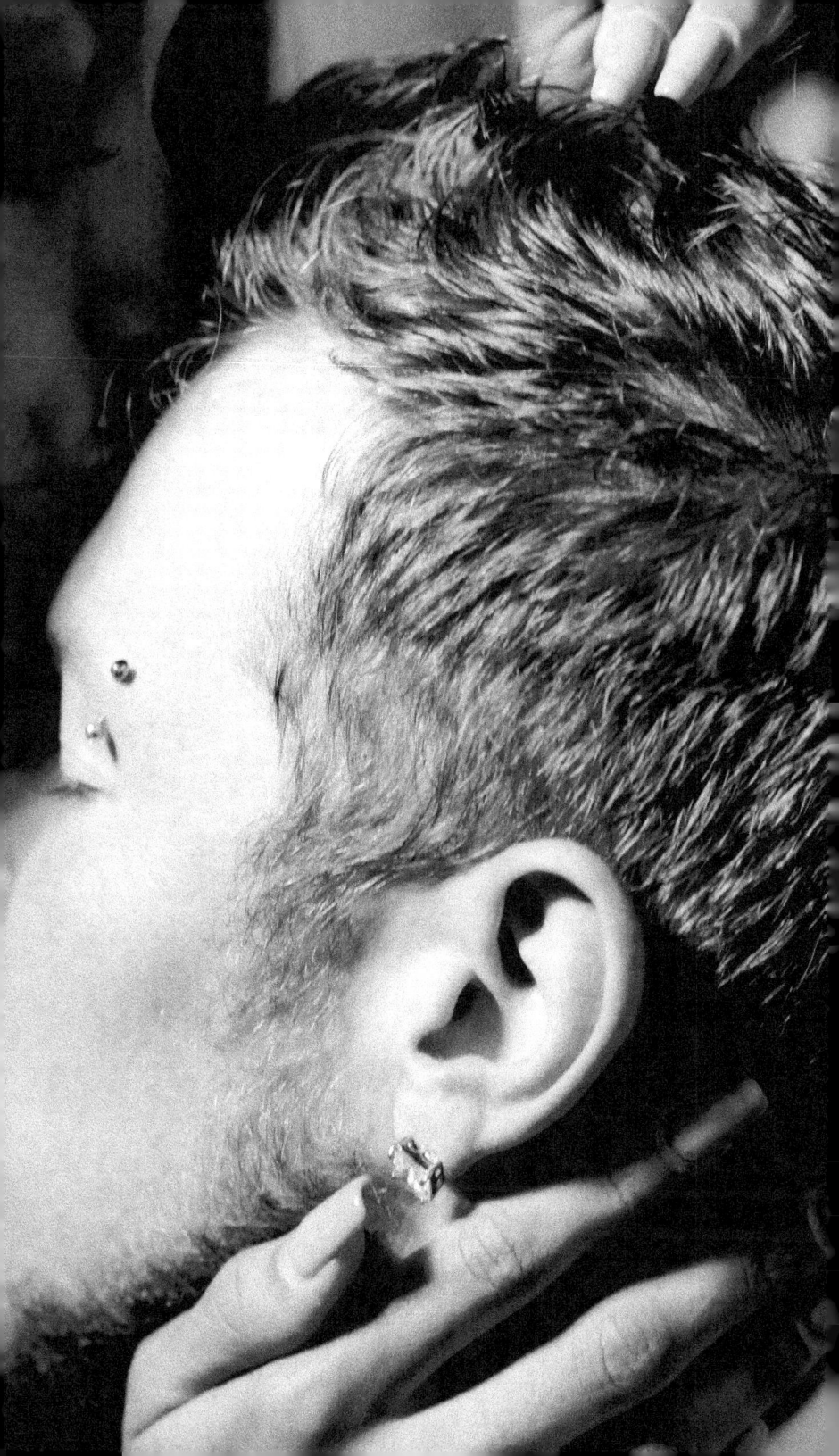

#021

Stop waiting for somebody
who is perfect.

They don't exist.

There is only somebody
who is perfect,
for you.

- Mark Anthony

#022

A healthy relationship
is based on love,
which is based on trust,
respect,
and clear communication,
especially when
times are hard.

- Mark Anthony

#023

When you meet the right one,
you'll understand
why it never worked
with anyone else.

It wasn't meant to be.

Until it's meant to be.

- Mark Anthony

#025

One day,
you'll look into someone's eyes
and realize,
this is the love
that was worth

every lonely *night*.

You will never
have to chase
who is meant
to knock on your door.

- *Mark Anthony*

#026

Through it all,
I've stayed,
not because
everything
was always perfect,
but because I saw
something in her
from the very start
that was worth
holding on to,
no matter
the weather.

- Mark Anthony

#027

Never apologize
for the fire inside you.

Let it burn.

Your inspiration
is exactly what
the world needs.

You are
a miracle,
just being you.

- *Mark Anthony*

#028

Kissing you
in the quiet slumber
of the afternoon,
tasting the sweetness
on your lips,
feeling your breathing
breaking
across my skin,
I can feel the world
disappearing around us,
as our souls,
and our hearts
and our bodies
become one,
as we disappear
again
into the quiet dream
of another afternoon.

- Mark Anthony

#029

I wanted to be the one
whose name you called
when you felt pleasure,
and when you
needed somebody
to understand
your pain.

— Mark Anthony

#030

Your body is like an ocean
I want to sail,
as bedsheets tangle with skin,
and our hands explore
the uncharted waters of desire
where breath and body
disappear like sunken treasures
beneath waves of pleasure,
waiting to be found again
and again and again.

- *Mark Anthony*

#031

You will not have to chase
what is meant for you.

True love comes
when you are walking your own
road
and they are walking theirs,
and suddenly
your roads meet
and go on
forever
in the same
direction.

— Mark Anthony

#032

I want to get lost in your
flames,
to feel myself
disappear into the delicate
embers of your mouth,
then to be reborn
into the ordinary light
of another day--
drinking a cup of coffee with

you,

and laughing
at the nothing we must endure
together,
before we disappear again
into the fire.

- *Mark Anthony*

#033

One day you will see
that the difference
between
love and lust,
and discover
lust only wants
the body,
but love wants
the body,
the mind,
and the soul.

- Mark Anthony

#034

True love
isn't built
on adolescent
fantasies
full of longing
and fantasy,
but a deeper
connection
that sees
beyond
the fantasy
into an endless
desire
for somebody's
company
that will last
longer
than infatuation,
a connection
that will stand
the test
of time.

- Mark Anthony

#035

When it rains
in the city,
don't run away.

Hold the one
you love,
and let
the rain
fall upon your faces.

Feel the moment
blessing you,
and let the rain
remind you
that forever
is made
of moments
like this.

— *Mark Anthony*

#036

You deserve so much more
than this world will tell you
with its dread and doom,
its plastic heart,
and eyes of only money.

You are not what the world
tells you.
You are a mountain,
a forest, an infinite sky.

You are a miracle
in human form,
a story
with a happy ending,
just waiting to be told

- Mark Anthony

#037

She's an angel
with a human heart,
and a devil's smile.

- Mark Anthony

#038

At the end of the day,
if someone cares about you,
they care about how their
actions impact you,
and make you feel.

That's all you need to know
about people,
and if you want them in your
life.

- *Mark Anthony*

\#039

If they are confused about you,
let them be confused,
and move on to find somebody
who can see clearly
what a rare treasure you are.

They are out there,
and they are waiting
for you.

– Mark Anthony

#040

The math is simple:

If you can't find somebody
who *loves*
all of you,
body, mind, and soul,
you are better off alone.

- Mark Anthony

#041

Tonight
your body
is as graceful
as moonlight
on the ocean,
and I want to get lost
in your fragrance.

I want to disappear
into the gentle waters
of your skin,
until we are
only memory,
and salt.

— *Mark Anthony*

#043

We were strangers
until one day,
love introduced us,
and said,
"I can see
you already
know each other."

– Mark Anthony

#044

Your most important
lessons
are the most painful ones
because without the pain,
you would do it over again,

and never *grow*
into the bad ass
you were truly meant
to be.

- *Mark Anthony*

#045

The problem is
you don't think love
exists anymore;
you think
the modern world
has stolen it,
with its smartphones,
and dating apps,
but nothing
can destroy love
because,
without it,
the world
would no longer exist.

So forget everything
they tell you,
and rest assured
love is real,
and it will find you
when you are
ready.

- Mark Anthony

#046

You must touch her heart
with your sincerity,
then find a way
to keep touching her,
and reminding her
that your love is real,
and that your love
is the only love
she has ever wanted,
and the only love
she will ever need.

- *Mark Anthony*

#047

You will never live up
to all the lies the
world tells you
about who you need to be
in order to be loved.

So love yourself as you are
right now,
flawed, confused,
and beautifully human,
and live your truth,
which is the only truth that
matters,
because it is the only truth
that can set you free.

— Mark Anthony

#048

Whatever darkness you're
running from,
whatever pain you
don't want to feel,
know that you're not alone.

Know that there is
somebody out there
who will understand your pain,
and want to take it from you.

Remember that good people
still exist,
and that they are the ones
who hold the world
together

just like *you.*

- Mark Anthony

#049

Sometimes
the universe
takes you
on a journey
you didn't know
you needed
in order to
bring you

everything
you
ever wanted.

- Mark Anthony

#050

There are so many ways
you captivate me,
with a story or a smile,
a touch, a gesture,
a look, a way of listening
deeply to every word I say,
because you can hear

yourself in my words,
and you know
there is nothing more
beautiful
than this.

- Mark Anthony

#051

love will love

all of your *imperfections,*
and scars,
and you will never need
to alter a photo
to make it look more beautiful
than it already is.

- Mark Anthony

#052

Don't hide
your naked body
from me.

Whatever flaws
and imperfections
you fear showing me,
are erased
by my desire
to devour all of you,
body, mind, scars,
and soul.

- Mark Anthony

#053

All of this advice
on how to heal from a broken
heart
when nothing matters,
until you look inside
to discover
it's not broken,
just in pain,
but once you have grieved
the pain,
you will feel whole again,
and life will continue
in a way
you didn't think was possible,
until you started living it.

- Mark Anthony

#054

You won't scare
the right one
by being real
because that is
exactly
what they've
been starving for.

- Mark Anthony

#055

Take off your clothes slowly,
and let this electricity
flow a little longer
through my veins,
as you reveal your
naked body
and soul to me
one button at a time.

Let your delicate fingers
walk along the shore
of my body,
teasing me slowly
and inevitably
into the trembling
ecstasy of us.

- Mark Anthony

#056

Let me devour you
with my mouth,
and taste the sweetness
of your skin,
listening for the delicate
moans of pleasure,
escaping your mouth
like a siren singing
just for me.

- Mark Anthony

#057

I love to ravish your body
in the still of the night,
to hear your breathing heavy,
as you give yourself to me
in the dark.

I don't want to control you.
I don't want to own you.
I want you to come to me
by your own free will,
and ask for me
to ravish you
in a gentle voice
so full of urgency
and fire,
the night
turns to ashes,
leaving nothing
but the memory
of us.

- Mark Anthony

#058

There will be days when you
miss each other,
even when they are right beside
you,
because life has a habit of
building walls
around our hearts,
but love always remembers
how to climb over them.

Love always finds a way back
to love.

- Mark Anthony

#059

Sometimes you heal
from a *broken heart*
by telling the same story
over and over,
until the pain weakens,
and the poison leaves,
so remember
that each time you
find the courage to speak
your truth,
you drive out the dark,
and a light comes in
to take its place.
Then you will see your past
scattered in the wind
like the pages
of an old book,
and when you look
closely you will find
these pages tell the story of
how you found
your happily ever after.

— Mark Anthony

#060

What is meant for you
will always feel natural,
calm and clear,
not forced,
chaotic or confusing.

That isn't what love
should feel like.

- Mark Anthony

#061

Stay still
and let me look at you.
Let me take in the curves
of your body,
the way your hair
falls around your shoulders
like water. Let me take
in your beauty
like art, like nature,
like you and only you.

- Mark Anthony

#063

Sometimes I miss her,
even when we are in the same
room.

I long for her to touch me,
open me, feed me, excite me,
with her words and body,
her laughter and her smile.

Tonight, there was an ocean
between us,
until you called my name,
and reached out your delicate
hand
to save me from myself.

How lucky I am to have you
so close and still so
in love.

- Mark Anthony

#064

She wants to love
that is rare,
honest and wild.

A heart that
isn't afraid
to love.

A soul
that isn't afraid
to dance.

- *Mark Anthony*

#065

Her body awakens
desire in me,
the way the spring
awakens the flowers,
and the moon awakens
the night.

- Mark Anthony

#066

One day,
 my dream
met your dream,
and together
we dreamed
a dream
of us,
and that dream
became true,
and so I have no use
for dreams now,
only you.

- Mark Anthony

#067

As much as I love her,
I still need time alone,
and so does she.

Time to remember who I am,
to feel the aching in the soul,
and the yearning in my heart.

I still need time alone
to remember who I am,
so that I can remember
why I love you,
and why I don't like to be
alone.

- Mark Anthony

#068

The way you tremble
when I touch you
reminds me how fragile
the space is
between
love and desire,
between
wanting and having
and
letting go.

- Mark Anthony

#069

When I softly touch your skin,
I can hear the music of your
soul,
and the more I listen,
the more I fall in love.

- Mark Anthony

#070

Come with me into this room
where I will strip for you,
and show you my naked soul,
so that if you desire me
I will know your desire
is true,
and should love come knocking
on the door, I promise
to let it in,
because I want you for all
times,
not just this time.

I want you again and again
and again.

- Mark Anthony

\#072

The sky opens
in your eyes,
and a million flowers
sway inside me
as your body brings my soul
into *Spring*
from a long, long winter
of wanting you.

— *Mark Anthony*

#073

Nothing compares
to the way
you give yourself to me,
the way you surrender your
body,
the tenderness, the strength,
the vulnerability,
and the power.

- Mark Anthony

#074

This moment, love,
is all we have,
so hold me closely,
devour me,
make me forget
the rest of the world exists,
and I will never leave you,
for there will be no place else
to go.

— Mark Anthony

\#076

There is an electricity I feel
when you touch me
that travels like lightning

through my body,

and leaves me trembling
with a desire to feel the rain.

- Mark Anthony

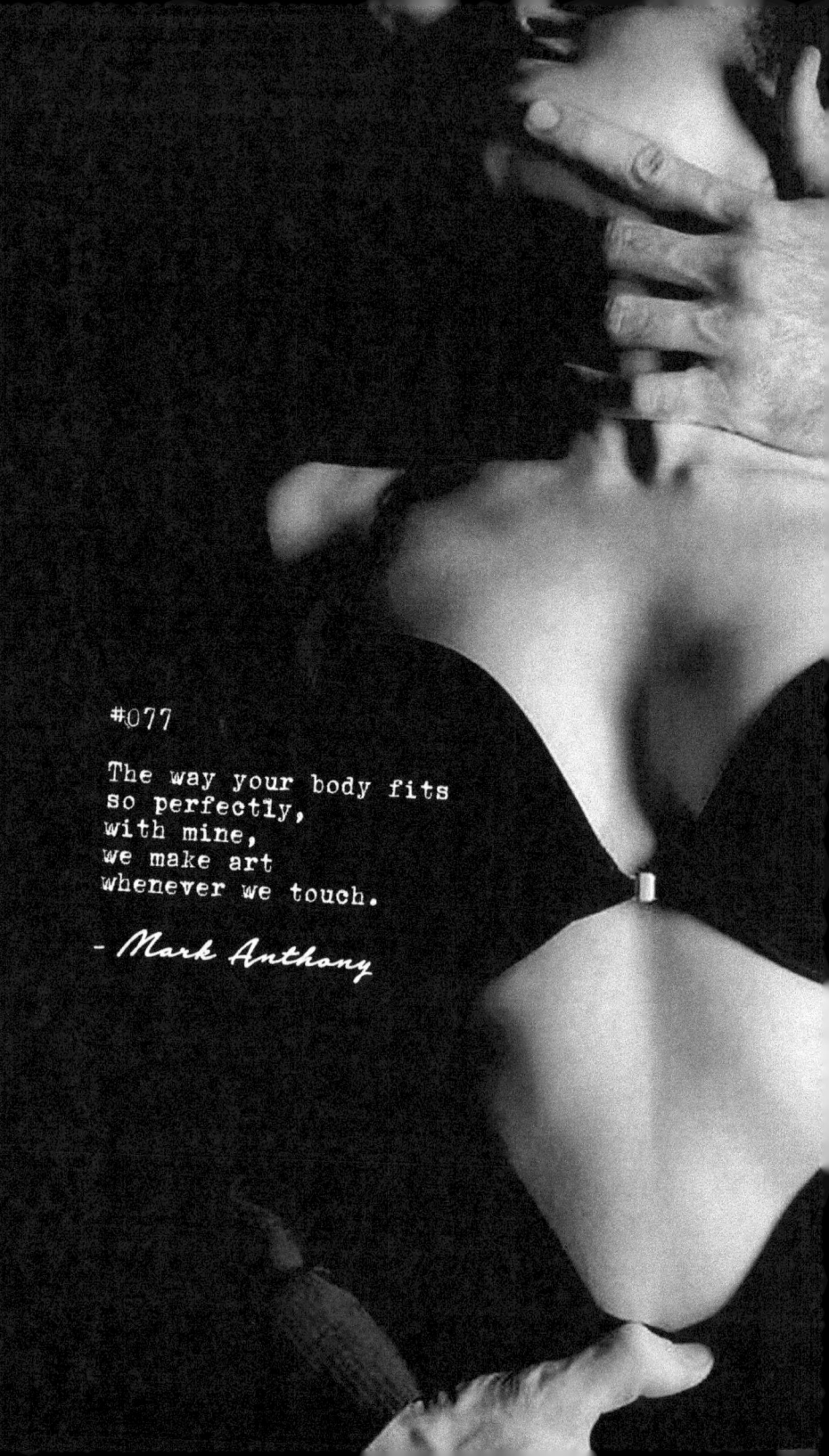

#078

I will never get tired
of exploring
the geography of your body,
with it's moonlit hills,
it's sun-drenched dunes,
it's dark forest of wet leaves
and wildflowers.

My desire for you
is an endless flame
setting fire to all
the vanities of earth,
and when I hold you tightly,
you are the entire universe,
breathing softy

in my arms.

- Mark Anthony

#079

I used to think poetry
was how beautifully you put
your feelings into words,
but now I think
it is how sincerely
they come *from the heart.*

- Mark Anthony

#081

If you want real love
get ready
to let go of your ego,
and be brave
because
you will have
to face
all of your insecurities.

You have to be naked,
and vulnerable,
with a heart
that is strong
enough for two.

- Mark Anthony

#082

You deserve a love that's real,
even on hard days.

You deserve a love that's chosen
on the daily
without questions or hesitation.

You deserve a soulmate,
strong enough
to handle your fire.

- Mark Anthony

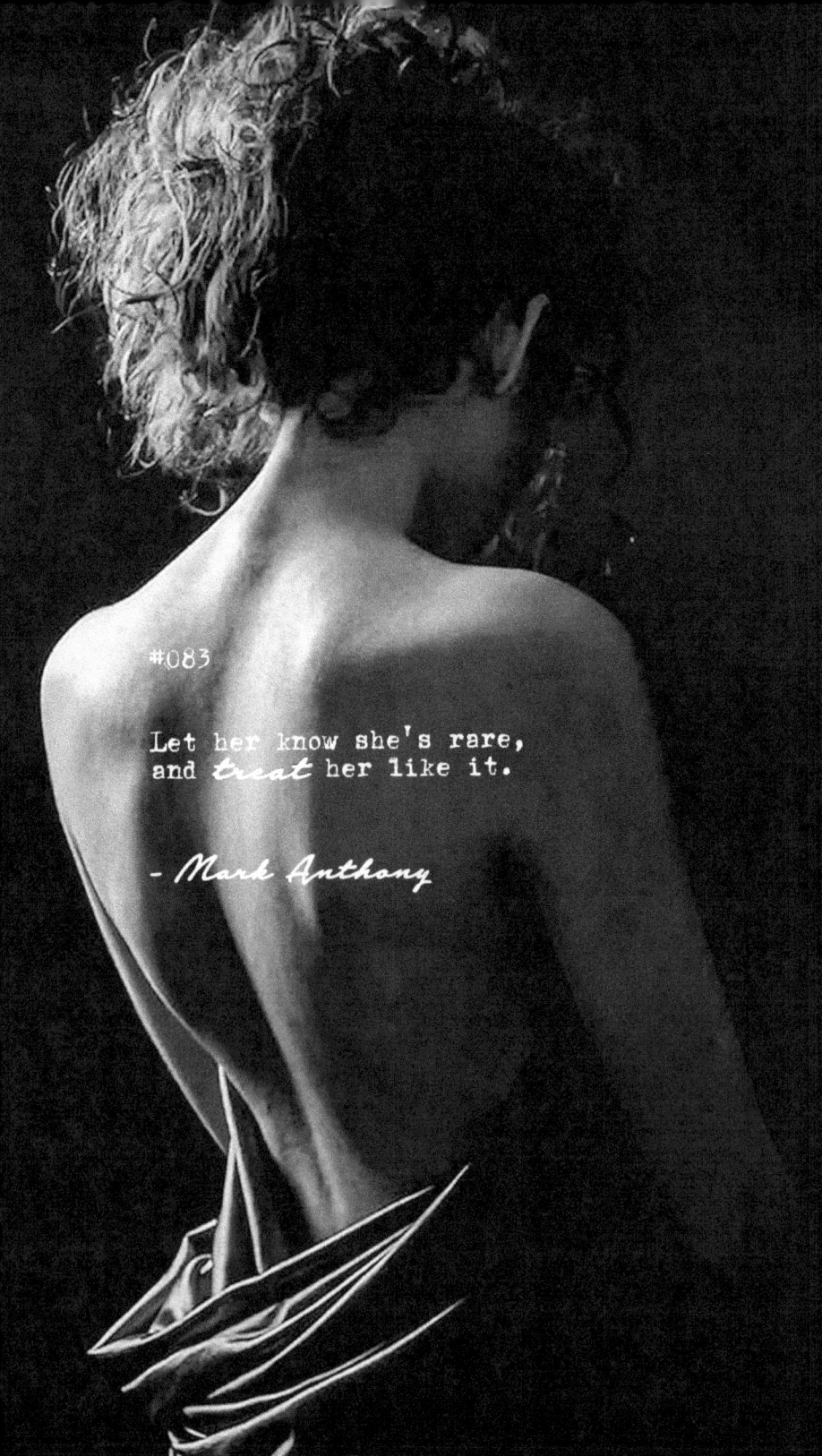

#084

Thinking of love
as a competition
is the beginning of the end.

I know she is the right one for
me,
and she knows I'm right for
her,
and in all the years
we've been together,
we've never forgotten this
simple truth.

- Mark Anthony

#085

There is always
the pressure
to live up to what
the world says
you should be,
but when we met
I knew the most
important thing
I had to offer her
was the courage
to be myself
in the face of

that *pressure.*

— Mark Anthony

\#086

```
Sometimes
you have to live it
to learn it,
and there is no other way,
so forgive yourself.
```

There was no other way.

— Mark Anthony

#087

You can read
a thousand poems
on how to heal your broken
heart,
but the only one
that matters,
is the one you write
with your actions
when you are ready to move on,
and by then, you will have no
need for poetry
because you will have become
the poem.

- Mark Anthony

#088

She's on fire,
fierce,
and unstoppable.

- Mark Anthony

#089

Watching you undress
like the ocean,
spreading across a sandy shore
and retreating back into the
infinite
from which you came.

With each button you
smile at me,
and with each snap of fabric,
you tease me like a child.

With each line of lace,
you erase me with your thumb,
and turn me into a thousand
shades of desire.

#090

Finding your soulmate
doesn't change
who you are.

It reminds you
of who
you've always been.

- Mark Anthony

#092

Her fire makes her fierce,
and *forever.*

– Mark Anthony

#093

We both know
if we'd met
at any other time
and place
in our lives,
it wouldn't have
worked
for countless
reasons,
so you can see why
timing is everything,
and why real love
is always always
worth the wait.

- Mark Anthony

#095

You must go beyond
desire and lust
in order to find love,
but if she's the one,
she will inspire
all of this,
and oh so much more.

- Mark Anthony

#096

There will never be
another pleasure
to compare with
covering you
in kisses,
in caresses,
in love,
to feeling you
pulling me closer,
and whispering dark secrets
in my ear.

This kind of miracle
is the only kind
of miracle I need
to know deep in my bones,
the world is magic,
in all its fire.

- Mark Anthony

#098

There is a flower
inside her heart
that can only be opened
by sincere words
spoken from the heart,
and when she smiles,
you will know
that flower
has bloomed.

- Mark Anthony

#099

Someone out there
is praying
to meet somebody

exactly like you.

Keep being yourself,
so that when they find you,
they'll know it's you,
and that they've finally found
the rare and unique soul
they've always been looking
for.

— *Mark Anthony*

#100

After all the years
you will spend running
from the truth in your soul,
one day you will look back
on this, as the years
you needed to suffer
and see that you are human,
and deserving
of so much more than suffering.

\#101

If I leave anything behind
that mattered,
it will be the way I
 loved you,
openly, honestly,
and bravely,
knowing you were
always
the one
I wanted to share
my life with,
the one
who made
my ordinary life,
forever an adventure.

- *Mark Anthony*

#103

I will always cherish
the gift
of holding you
in the quiet dark,
your body pressed against mine
like a flower inside a book,
your perfume still takes me
to Paris,
and shows me a painting
of two lovers
rising above the city
like purple clouds,
and from this dream
I never want to wake,
and if this is us,
I know it has always been us,
and will forever be us,
if ever there was an us

in the *universe.*

- Mark Anthony

to be continued...

You can read more of my work on
Facebook and Instagram:
@markanthonypoet
or visit me at
www.markanthonypoet.com

*Also by
Mark Anthony*

the poetry of us | twin flames
dream | soulmates 1 & 2
love notes | true love
a beautiful life

www.ingramcontent.com/pod-product-compliance
Lightning Source LLC
Chambersburg PA
CBHW052149070526
44585CB00017B/2034